SHAPESHIFTER

SHAPESHIFTER

poetry and prose by

L.E. Bowman

Button Publishing Inc.
Minneapolis
2025

SHAPESHIFTER
POETRY
AUTHOR: L.E. Bowman
COVER DESIGN: Coral Black

◇

◇

Published by Button Poetry
Minneapolis, MN 55418 | http://www.buttonpoetry.com

◇

Manufactured in the United States of America
PRINT ISBN: 978-1-63834-118-5
EBOOK ISBN: 978-1-63834-119-2

Second printing

For my pot of gold.

CONTENTS

5 Shapeshifter

6 Life Doesn't Ask Permission

7 Have You Ever Looked at Yourself and Not Blinked

8 Are You Enough for You is the Only Question You Need to Answer

9 What Can You Do About It?

10 My Peloton Instructor Tells Me to Silence my Soft Side

11 We All Have the Same Hours in the Day

12 Hope You're Okay, and Even if You Aren't, You Can Just Be

13 To Be a *Good* Woman

14 To Be a *Good* Man

15 My Mom Reminds Me That We All Have Our Shit

16 Billions of Suns Afraid of the Dark

17 More Lamp than Sun

18 Red

19 When Two People Seem So Perfect For Each Other

20 It Hurts a Lot and then It Doesn't

21 Fire-Raiser

22 No Man's Land

23 All Heart and No Break

24 What Do You Need?

25 A Good Cry

26 "...tender like a bruise"

27 Hesitation

28 bal·ance

29 *Billions of Cicadas Emerge After 17 Years Underground*

30 Live Before You Die

31 There is What You Think You Are, and then There is More

32 Outlast

33 Let Them Miss You

34 Just Call Me the Rose of Jericho

35 I Have Been Both Ocean and Desert

36 "I Know Love Returns Because Flowers Do"

37 You Move

38 Just Show Up

39 A Little Wrecked

40 Hope Is

41 What I Mean to Say Is

42 What Does it Mean to Have a Life Well Lived?

43 Oh Love, You Finicky Little Bitch

44 He Tells Me He Isn't Attracted to Older Women

45 Are You on Your ~~Period~~ *Bullshit*?

46 The Worst Could Happen, But

47 Life is Soup, I am Fork

48 Little Rescues

49 The Body Knows

50 More Than One Way to Move the Needle

51 "Some men think…"

52 My Mom Says that Everyone Should Take Their Shoes Off

53 To-Do List

54 You're So ~~Pretty~~ *Unruly*

55 Inside Job

56 "There is No Remedy for Love but to Love More"

57 Stay

58 My Husband Asks Why I Never Write About Him

59 The Dirt Always Knows

61 Old Friend

62 A Promise

63 You Don't Say *I Love You* Often

64 Slow Living

65 Common Miracles

66 Salt

67 Matrescence

69 This is the Unedited Version

70 *You Handle Postpartum So Well*

71 Soft, White Underbelly

72 Lover

73 Precious

74 How Much Do I Love You?

75 What Love We Have Left

76 Motherhood

77 Empty

78 I'm Sorry If We Don't Leave You Anything Worth Having

79 I Would Say that I Wish Our Currency Was Flowers

80 Isn't Every Day the End of the World for Someone?

81 On the Days You Feel Less Than

82 "I'm Eggshell Fine: Currently Whole but Easily Crushed"

83 Love is Complicated

84 A Stranger on the Street Returns a Smile

85 Dolce Far Niente

86 I Want to Stay Young Forever

87 Newborn

88 Mother

89 All of These Are True

90 Put Your Own Oxygen Mask on First

91 Especially When

92 "The Longer I Live the More Beautiful Life Becomes"

94 An Anthem for My C-Section Scar After Childbirth

95 I'll Stop Writing About Loving My Body

96 I Won't Call You Pretty

97 Joy Harjo said, "the heart is the smaller cousin of the sun"

98 "Love yourself. Then forget it. Then love the world."

99 The Thing About Tragedy

100 The Best of You

101 Invisible Work

102 "You don't always have to be graceful"

103 A Reader Rolls Her Eyes

104 "How can I begin anything new with all of yesterday in me?"

105 You Create Your Life as You Move

107 Break and Make it Beautiful

108 Whatever It Takes

109 I Know I am a Mother

110 The State of Your House is the State of Your Mind

111 My Son Brings Me Things That He Finds Interesting

112 The Closer You Step to the Edge, the More Beautiful the View

113 Come as You Are

114 I Love My Body

115 The Greatest Gift I Can Give My Daughter

116 Happiness

117 Adulting (*It's Called Balance, Darling*)

118 Chaotic Good

119 Silience

120 I Will Swallow the Sun

122 *"Aging is an extraordinary process..."*

123 Home

124 You Can Keep Your Sapling Body

125 A New Kind of Sexy

126 I Woke Up Today

127 If You're Alive, Then Act Alive

128 "All Good Things are Wild and Free"

129 Pregnancy After Miscarriage

130 A Woman on Instagram Says She Can Help Me Stay Small

131 Woman Might Be a Science, but It's Also an Art

132 Feral Housewife

133 This is Going to Be an Ordinary Life

134 Maybe We Should Give All the Fucks

135 When I Die

136 My Pot of Gold

139 Acknowledgements

141 About the Author

143 Author Book Recommendations

149 Credits

SHAPESHIFTER

SHAPESHIFTER

At any given moment
there are at least 2,000 storms happening on Earth,
and today I am one of them.
I am less than I used to be, but somehow more than
I ever was.
Let's not talk of rebellions, even if this feels
like the greatest rebellion of them all.
The anger hasn't left me, but it's finally controlled.
Have you ever felt so sure of who you are,
but no longer recognize the face looking back at you?
Each stretch of life requires a new form,
and the in between is shaky ground.
The other side is calling, but what will it be?
There is always a struggle,
something this wild will always try to escape.
Are we all just shapeshifters unable to settle
into a shape?

LIFE DOESN'T ASK PERMISSION

How do you welcome a chapter you aren't ready for?
  A birth. A death.
  A moment that changes everything.
How do you let go of old definitions?
  No longer feel the same ache.
  No longer pull joy from the same things.
How do you move in a new body?
  Learn to love with a heart that is intimate with pain.
  Learn to embrace bones and skin that are altered by age.
How do you accept that life is always moving,
  that nothing can remain the same?

HAVE YOU EVER LOOKED AT YOURSELF AND NOT BLINKED?

Yesterday it rained, but today the sun is shining.
There is a lesson in there somewhere, but my mind is too fogged
to know what it is.
I've checked all the boxes, made all the lists.
When I sit down, I have to unbutton my pants to breathe.
When I stand, my legs move in circles and my head spins.
The only breakroom I can step into smells like broccoli and
microwaved fish.
When everything turns off, all you're left with are reactions,
all you have in your hands are anger and indifference.
How many ways can I say *I'm tired*.
How many times can the world respond with *get over it*.
My heart is a canary, and I've been ignoring the screams.
How long before her breath gives out completely.

Last night I cried in the shower.
This morning I smeared something sickening-sweet under my eyes
and practiced smiling until even I was convinced.

ARE YOU ENOUGH FOR YOU IS THE ONLY QUESTION YOU NEED TO ANSWER

I've always managed to be soft
with other people.
It is with myself
that I lose the ability
to forgive.

WHAT CAN YOU DO ABOUT IT?

toss your phone out of the window / put the music, the rage, on display / scream like you're singing / stop pretending / meet your ghost halfway / expand until you can feel it / let your senses settle into the moment / describe the taste, the texture, the sight, the sound / understand that it's a long road back to yourself / accept who you are – *truly* / acknowledge the discomfort – *fully* / let go of the shame

admit self-loathing is a corpse that won't ever decay

MY PELOTON INSTRUCTOR TELLS ME TO SILENCE MY SOFT SIDE, LET THE STRONG SIDE SPEAK

But it's the strong in me that is gasping for breath,
shaking as she trudges up this mountain.
But it's the strong in me that can barely stand.

This is where tired lies – behind my smile.
Some days I'm drowning and today the water is high.
  My ceiling stars are peeling off.
  My heart is pounding in my skull.
They say that chaos brings transformation,
but I'm tethered to this ocean floor just watching the light dance.

I can't relax without collapsing.
I can't sigh without losing my breath.
There is a woman in me crying already.
She's the one I've silenced.
She's the one brave enough to give in.

WE ALL HAVE THE SAME HOURS IN THE DAY

Oh do we, Ashley?
Go get your ten thousand steps.
Let me have some peace.

HOPE YOU'RE OKAY, AND EVEN IF YOU AREN'T, YOU CAN JUST BE

I.

There are no easy answers for love, for grief.
For hating your job but needing the money.
For still wanting a lover who no longer wants you.

There are no easy answers for loneliness, for discontent.
For spending time with people who don't really know you.
For fighting the world because the anger is easier to hold onto.

There are no easy answers for disappointment, for fatigue.
For wondering *why* because your last attempts amounted to nothing.
For the days you're dragging your body around as you go.

II

The truth is, survival is easy, but living is not.
The truth is, happiness is fragile.
The truth is, peace is even more so.
There are a thousand ways to die,
most as common and understated as a shallow breath.
They take you, slowly.
A cat with nine lives who doesn't know
how many are left.

III

I took a hot bath today. Tossed lavender and eucalyptus into the steaming water, rubbed salt across my shoulders and legs. Later, thick lotion and sweet wine. Later still, deep breaths of night air. The tang of honeysuckle, and the musk of smoke. I watched as the birds settled in for the night. Heard the faint call of an owl rising.

There is more than pain in the world, isn't there?
There is more than joy.
There is life leaping into darkness, wings out, soaring.

TO BE A *GOOD* WOMAN

You must breathe sacrifice.
Be a worthy daughter, sister, friend *before, before, before.*
You must hold your anger in your jaw until it turns
into a smile.
Be strong in the softest way.
Slight, but with ample curves to fill wanting hands.
You must *bend, bend, bend*, but if you break,
make it a thing of beauty.
Your arms must be open, but not reaching.
Your body is made for giving, not receiving.

You must need to be saved, but not needy.
A worthwhile chase (*but begging to be tamed*).
Quiet.
Straightlaced.

Apologize. Apologize. Apologize.
Down on your knees, chin raised.

TO BE A *GOOD* MAN

You must guzzle gasoline.
Be a leader, provider, protector *before, before, before.*
You must hold your fear in your chest until it turns
into anger.
Let it be the fire that burns you for years.
You must be a force, but not threatening.
Stoic, but warm enough to feel like a home.
You must *want, want, want*, but if you need,
make it a thing of hunger.
You're a lover, but you don't need to be loved.

You must sever the soft parts from your body.
Create a steel spine.
Be steady.
All-knowing.

Suppress. Suppress. Suppress.
Show no weakness, man-up.

MY MOM REMINDS ME THAT WE ALL HAVE OUR SHIT

Which is to say, we've all stepped in some form of feces,
all found ourselves rubbing our shoes on a random sidewalk,
trying to ignore the stench.
Which is to say, be kind.
You never know what sores are festering on the flesh we keep hidden.
You never know what crap we've been dropped into,
what soft core sits just below our hard rinds.
Aren't we all fruit, really?
Glossy peels concealing the discolored, mushy inside,
 our raw parts, our open wounds.
Aren't we all wedged between teeth,
just waiting to be consumed?

Remember, the things that bring us together
are the things we often keep to ourselves.
Remember, it's the ugly that we have in common,
the rot, the blood, and the bruise.

BILLIONS OF SUNS AFRAID OF THE DARK

Maybe there is so much smoke because we are all on fire.
Maybe we feel like we are standing alone because we
can't see past our own hands.
The air burns when we breathe, and we can't pull our eyes
from the ground.
If there is anything that links us all together, it's this.
We set ourselves aflame and call it light.
We burn and call it warmth.
A world of stars on the brink of exploding.
Billions of suns afraid of the dark.

MORE LAMP THAN SUN

A murmuration of starlings dances above me,
and I wonder what it feels like to truly belong.
I think my heart is more lamp that sun;
    my light seems dimmer these days.
Easily smothered. Easily snuffed out.
I put up walls and thought I built a home,
but I'm more prisoner than homemaker,
more trapped than free.
I spent years wishing I was fragile enough to love.
Now, I exist as a delicious combination of fear and reckless need,
    a bird with an open cage.
To jump into uncertainty, or to stay confined...

I think about the wildness of nature,
    the longing, the ache.
I know that one day the sun will feel warm again.
I know that belonging can be redefined.

I refuse to be a victim.
I won't abandon my life.

RED

It's easy to step back now and see the whole picture.
It's easy to pick out all the signs we missed and hate ourselves
for doing so.
They were obvious, weren't they? Red and flashing.
But isn't passion the same color as blood?
How easy it is to convince ourselves we see something
that isn't there.
Dreamers, the lot of us.
Hopefuls, casting wishes to distant stars while ignoring
the glaring sun.

But can we be blamed after being blinded by such light?
I still have spots in my eyes from my time with you.
I can still feel the warmth of your touch.

WHEN TWO PEOPLE SEEM SO PERFECT FOR EACH OTHER, WHY CAN'T THEY OVERCOME THE CIRCUMSTANCES PULLING THEM APART?

In another life, we lay in bed and talk finances.
And talk kids.
And talk buying rocking chairs for our new front porch.
In another life, you quiet the whispers of your spirit, and I continue
carving out my heart.

In another life, the world isn't bigger than
we are.

IT HURTS A LOT AND THEN IT DOESN'T

We all worship something –
 even the ocean breathes for the moon.
And how many beds does she crawl into each night?
How many hearts does she promise to hold?
I don't want to be your grey sky, but I know
I can't be your light.

The heart is a hand,
 open and reaching or balled tight.

The mind is a wanderer,
 always hungry, never satisfied.

Dreams are endless,
 even with open eyes.

This life will kill you,
 again and again.

FIRE-RAISER

The day ate me alive, or maybe I ate myself.
Bad attitudes are like oil in a hot pan.
Everything spits fire. Everything burns.
But who's to blame? The pan? The oil?
My hands that are now blistering and painful?
My mouth that is now breathing flames?
Was the day already burning, or did I set it on fire?

NO MAN'S LAND

I'm tired of looking for meaning.
Existence.
Purpose.
Why the river keeps storms from finding their way to this
spit of desert I'm currently living in.
Why the trees sound like a hundred rattlesnakes shaking their tails,
and the sun feels like she's inching closer.
White light burning. Unforgiving heat.
Where is the darkness to hide in?
Cool, damp earth?
I would dig a hole and crawl inside, but I fear the ground
is already too dry.
Where do I go from here?
How do I find the rain?

ALL HEART AND NO BREAK

I know you yearn. I know you hunger. I recognize that forsaken look in your eyes because I've seen it in mine. Let's stop ignoring the growls. Let's stop pretending that this longing isn't supposed to be felt. The earth isn't pearl-white and clean – she's tainted and dirty. She sweats, she cries, she screams. We're supposed to expand when life is growing, so why do we keep asking ourselves to shrink? Let's shake off our shackles the way the morning shakes off the night. With a heart that burns orange-yellow. With the desire for an uninhibited life.

WHAT DO YOU NEED?

A long dip in crystal clear water. The ocean. The mountains. The serenity you find among the trees. A vacation. A day. A moment away. A good, long kiss and a love letter. A shoulder to lean on. A hand, gentle and steady. A heart that is ready. Someone who stops long enough to truly see. A large bowl of soup, salty and steaming. An open window. A warm blanket. A kiss on the forehead you can feel for weeks. Time to heal. Time to feel. Love. Support. Acceptance. Some much-needed clarity. The lingering touch of another human. The healing energy of the earth at your feet. A partner to share life with. Steady arms to dance with. A map. A sign. Some sense of direction.

A hug. A hug. A hug.
Peace. Peace. Peace.

A GOOD CRY

In your office bathroom when a coworker questions
how you're feeling.
While folding laundry, your mind still working and moving
because your list is too long for a storm to slow you down.
On the floor where you landed.
At the table with wine as your only companion.
In the mess staring back at you from that chair in the
corner of your house.

Sitting in your driveway, engine off, heart running.
During that one commercial, that one movie,
that one song.

When a friend finally asks *what's wrong?*

Late at night, darkness around you,
sinking into the comfort
of your own arms.

"...TENDER LIKE A BRUISE"

— Marie Rutkoski

held like a grudge
burned like a bridge
oozing like a wound

tired like an early morning
fading like the evening light
pulled like an ocean tide

waiting like a distant lover
healing like a cut scabbed over
hopeful like an open door

reflective like the moon

HESITATION

My heart is a stone sunk in the bottom of a riverbed.
Unmoving save for the sheer will of another force slowly
pushing it along.
Think of the progress I would make if I was less hardened ground
and more beating flesh – gleaming, and wide-eyed, and free.
Yes, there is more to fear.
The kingfisher now watches me from a branch and there are
deeper waters calling.
Maybe I will get plucked and forced down a gullet
– *but think of the feeling.*
Think of the fear, and the instinct, and the fight to go on.
Maybe life isn't about escaping, maybe it's about succumbing.
Yielding to the one truth of life – that it all ends.
Even this mass I am on will one day explode or vanish into nothing.
But it's here now, isn't it?
Why am I not outside giving myself to the sun?
Why am I not singing?
Why am I not following this silver serpent of hope
out to the sea?

BAL·ANCE

noun an even distribution of weight enabling someone or something to remain upright and steady

I'm learning to be the eye
of my hurricane.
To be the calm in my chaos.
To spin, and crash, and break,
and still be at peace.

BILLIONS OF CICADAS EMERGE AFTER 17 YEARS UNDERGROUND

I want to write words that sing,
but how can I when I myself am barely breathing?
I know something of holding air in my lungs but nothing of
creating song.
Do you think a tree knows every leaf it carries?
The full extent of its roots?
I dream of the parts of myself I cannot feel.
I dream there is still more of me to be found.
Maybe there is something buried deep.
Maybe those occasional flutters in that foreign place inside of me
are its limbs stirring, its lungs pushing against restraints as it
attempts to find its breath.

The news today spoke of cicadas breaking through the ground.
Their tiny bodies crawling through the dark towards
a light they've never known.
I dream now of the darkness around me and the sky calling.
I shuffle towards it slowly, humming softly as I go.

LIVE BEFORE YOU DIE

The life you want isn't at the end of your fingertips,
it isn't beyond the horizon or the sky.
It's in the center of your palm waiting to be clutched.
It's on your tongue waiting to be tasted.
It's in the reverie you see every night in the shadows on your wall.
The one you can't remember to forget because you relive it
every time you close your eyes.

Do you hear your heart beating?
That's its voice.

Do you feel your stomach tightening?
That's its lungs trying to expand.

Dreams aren't meant to be whispers,
you have to scream them,
and beginnings start with darkness, not light.
Are you ready to create your own bright morning?
Are you ready to live before you die?

THERE IS WHAT YOU THINK YOU ARE, AND THEN THERE IS MORE

Do you think a baby bird, naked and blank-eyed,
knows that one day it will fly?
Does it already feel its wings unfolding?
Does its mother shout as she helps food down its throat,
    look up, the sky lies open,
or does life just do what life does?

One day it meets the sun for the first time,
the next a world of green.
And later still, the vast blue of endless possibility.

OUTLAST

I thought the stars would dim when you left,
but I'm sitting where we sat, looking up at the same sky,
and they are still bright.
And my god,
    are they just as beautiful as they were that night.
And my god,
    does the world still seem just as endless.
And my god,
    I promise to shine as long as they do.

LET THEM MISS YOU

Let them wonder what wild joy you're chasing,
  why you didn't think to invite them along.
Let them hear your laughter from afar,
watch as it pulls the sun from the sky,
  marvel at how easily you become that light.
Let them yearn to be your moon,
long for a chance to reflect the warmth you provide,
  admire how you can be so vibrant and alive without
  them beside you.

Let them miss you.
Let yourself learn how okay you are
on your own.

JUST CALL ME THE ROSE OF JERICHO

Because I too turned dry and shriveled,
collapsed into myself,
remained dormant during the relentless heat.

Because I too waited for the rain,

found renewal through my own restraint,
unfurled to show the world that rebirth is possible
when conviction and strength
meet hope.

I HAVE BEEN BOTH OCEAN AND DESERT:
I'D RATHER SPEND MY LIFE DROWNING, THAN ANOTHER DAY BEGGING FOR A DROP OF RAIN

The sun whispers to me in a golden voice,
but I'm choosing to focus on the sliver of moon
clinging to her portion of the sky.
The dark can't contain her, and I find a connection
with that beautiful truth.
We are both where we should be but still out of place,
both hiding parts of ourselves but still unafraid.
I will not die in a house like this,
a nail jammed into swelling wood,
bending in a direction I do not want to go.
I am half blind and half seeing.
Half starving and half too full to move.
Maybe I should seek the advice of fortune tellers,
of crystal balls, of painted cards.
Oh hope, do you mind if I join you?
I want to move towards soft, embracing places.
I want to wash this blood off in the sea.

"I KNOW LOVE RETURNS BECAUSE FLOWERS DO"

— Luke Levi

Because the old pecan tree still sprouts new leaves after lightning,
after burning.
Because cut stems can grow their own roots with a little water,
a little light.
Because last summer I tossed the bouquet you gave me
into the garbage, gathered seeds,
planted my own garden.
Because after several dark, heavy months,
their fresh faces finally looked to the sky.

YOU MOVE

I'm tired of writing about you.
It's a boring topic when a storm has just passed
and the air is thick and sweet.
The trees hang heavy with water, and the sun reflects on each leaf
like a thousand glimmering lights.
I could sit here in this desert of memories
until I am crisp and shriveled,
or I could step outside into something new.
I could sink into the green of your eyes,
or I could see that the grass is greener still.
I could dream of your needy hands,
or I could shiver at the air's delicate fingers
brushing against my skin.

How do you break chains you cannot see?
How do you free yourself from something that isn't there?
You move. You move.

JUST SHOW UP

Just show up. Even angry.
Even if you're smiling through your teeth
like a shark.
Even if it's all fake.
Even if the optimism and hope are just clothes
you can't wait to take off at the end of the day.

Just show up. Even unprepared.
Even insecure and unsteady.
Even fumbling and needing help.
Even if your ocean is so deep that you're lost
in yourself.

Just show up. Even tired.
Even wearing yesterday's stains on your clothes
and yesterday's dirt on your hands.
Ignore the side eyes that don't understand.
These things are easier for some people.
People who don't realize how close we all are
to the ground.
People who've never had to pull themselves out.

A LITTLE WRECKED

They say that the moon was once part of the earth.
A broken piece forced from her mother's body
and cast into darkness.
But look at her now – perfect and glowing. Whole.
Something once scattered newly formed.
Something once wrecked now complete on her own.
Aren't we all a little scattered? A little wrecked?
I look at her and see hope.

HOPE IS

fight. Is grit. Is bare knuckles bleeding.
Hope is missing nails and skin and teeth.
Hope is an oozing knee.
Hope isn't gentle.
Hope isn't kind.
Hope is a rushing river daring you to enter.
Hope is the ocean.
Hope is an endless grey sky.

WHAT I MEAN TO SAY IS

Look inward,
What I mean to say is, you are the answer to every question.
What I mean to say is, your life is the only one you can live.

Live outward.
What I mean to say is, your energy is healing.
What I mean to say is, your heart is a tiny sun, and this world
is cold enough as it is.

Stay in the moment.
What I mean to say is, we are and then we aren't.
What I mean to say is, the universe is a fickle mistress, and she takes
as much as she gives.

Open your arms.
What I mean to say is, we are all just trying to make it.
What I mean to say is, love exists in the simplest of moments.
  A hand reaching for another.
  A smile. Laughter.
  A kiss.

WHAT DOES IT MEAN TO HAVE A LIFE WELL LIVED?

I've seen death recently.
It's always been there with its claws and its teeth,
but I hear the growls now. I see the eyes.
It waits,
   – not touching, just reminding –
   nothing is promised, nothing is guaranteed.
Even this breath could shatter.
Even this exhale could be the last.

There are truths that the rocks and the roots know:
   the rot finds us all.
   the changing tides wear us down.
But even the ordinary has color, doesn't it?
   Bright and piercing.
   Dark and deep.
Even a fleeting moment can move us beyond belief.

I saw a live oak recently, surely over five hundred years old.
Branches twisted and reaching, stretching both up and down.
Pulling herself to the stars and sinking into the ground.
How many storms has she danced in?
How much life has she witnessed with her slow-blinking eyes?
What are years to her but a collective string of moments?
What is time?

Perhaps she holds the answer.

Will you slow down with me?
Will you acknowledge this one life we have to live?
I want this moment to linger.
I want this memory to sink into my skin.

OH LOVE, YOU FINICKY LITTLE BITCH

If only finding yourself was as easy as looking in a mirror.
If only loving yourself was as easy as not turning away.
These fingers are brittle, and these thoughts cut as they move.
If the past truly speaks, mine is screaming.
It's amazing how easily a lover can take the best parts of you
when they leave.
It's amazing how easily you can believe that they were all
those best parts.
How do you create happiness with empty hands?
We have to be more than hunger. More than longing.
We can't just exist to want.

I was told once that love will teach us all the ways
to die.
If this is true, I pray it will also teach us all the ways
to live again.

HE TELLS ME HE ISN'T ATTRACTED TO OLDER WOMEN

The swamp hag in me is singing, her 30-something tits swinging as she moves. One less intruder to trouble her sanctuary. One less set of hands trying to caress her sagging skin. Her crow's feet deepen with each passing moment, the creases around her lips continue to expand. I feed her until her double chin, triples. I toss her hairbrush, her tweezers in the trash. We grasp hands and run into the forest together, dance naked under the waxing moon. We celebrate this new discovery, that a woman can exist beyond the want of a man.

ARE YOU ON YOUR ~~PERIOD~~ *BULLSHIT?*

You're acting like ~~your mother~~ *Gaia freed from her cage.*
You seem a little ~~crazy~~ *feral*, just ~~calm down~~ *let yourself rage.*
You're ~~cute~~ *powerful* when you're angry.
You're strong ~~for a girl~~ *when you're unleashed.*
You should try ~~smiling~~ *unmasking your feelings.*
You should try ~~losing~~ *gaining* some ~~weight~~ *boundaries.*
~~Sweetheart~~. *Warrior.*
~~Honey~~. *Heroine.*
Just ~~stand there~~ *keep fighting* and ~~look pretty~~ *be.*

THE WORST COULD HAPPEN, BUT

after William Stafford

Surely, each day takes us closer to the end.

There is always destruction just around the corner,
troubled waters lapping our toes,
tendrils of fire licking our skin,
ruin waiting on the other side of this fading sun.

But what of the laughter I hear through the darkness?
What of the joy I feel right now?
This sweet, warm breath I'm taking.
This purple, orange sky I'm sitting under.
This incessant hope I'm clinging to.

LIFE IS SOUP, I AM FORK

And I wonder why the days are dribbling down my chin,
settling into the newly formed wrinkles
on my throat.
And I wonder why I am so tired.
The tedium of trying and missing, trying and missing,
trying and missing.
How long can you go empty before you become savage?
I think I feel the fangs emerging already.
I think I hear the wind whispering my name.
I think I'll skip life's prescribed duties and swim naked,
wash away these failures and disrupt these echoing days.
Why do I need utensils when I have hands?
Why do I need permission to do as I please?
I'm tired of starving;
today I'll pull the bowl to my lips and feast.

LITTLE RESCUES

coffee / sunlight / a smile / a laugh
a kiss on the forehead / a call from a friend
one of those lingering hugs that mothers give
the first hint of fall / the first touch of spring
any sign that change is coming
water / nature / a long, steaming bath
soft, gentle lips / open, familiar hands
a home cooked meal
a deep, cleansing breath
flowers / forgiveness / movement
rest
music – especially if it inspires you to dance

THE BODY KNOWS

Have you ever had a vacant mind, but a body full of feeling?
I want to laugh and cry at the same time.
I want to hold your hand as you point out all of the things
that are beautiful.
I want to be reminded that they still exist.
When the world is spinning around you, how do you
keep yourself from becoming dizzy?
Do you focus on one spot at a time?
I think I'm moving through another extinction.
I could be happy *if*, and *if*, and *if*, and *if*.
I'm tired of standing on the edge of something wild.
I want to step inside.
When the wind blows, I no longer want to close my shutters.
I want to open myself to the storm.
The truth is always there, it just doesn't always reveal itself.
The body knows, though, if you listen.
The heart, especially.
The heart and the hands.
The heart when it hums instead of beats.
The hands when they forget what they seek.

MORE THAN ONE WAY TO MOVE THE NEEDLE

There are more trees on Earth than stars in our galaxy,
and I am no longer ashamed of standing still.
The company I keep is beautiful and plenty,
is secure, is steady, is still expanding.
Can't you see? We do move.
Our roots reach and spread and intertwine
with others.
Our branches twist and expand always seeking
the light.
What's more hopeful than finding joy where
you're planted?
What's more magical than finding your own way
to touch the sky?

"SOME MEN THINK WOMEN WANT MONEY, CARS, AND GIFTS. BUT THE RIGHT WOMAN WANTS A MAN'S TIME, EFFORT, PASSION, HONESTY, LOYALTY, SMILE, AND HIS CHOOSING TO PUT HER AS HIS PRIORITY."

— *Charles Orlando*

And cheese. And good wine.
And a cottage deep in the woods where she can dance
naked under the moon, unbothered,
where she can swim in the cool water of a stream
without hungering eyes.
And a life without mirrors – let her fingers be
the only tool she has to judge her body.
Let the caress of her palms be the only language
her skin understands.

MY MOM SAYS THAT EVERYONE SHOULD TAKE THEIR SHOES OFF, STICK THEIR TOES IN THE EARTH

We are just animals, anyway. Meant to be barefoot and sun-kissed. Meant to be windblown and bug-bit. This disconnect is our own doing. We built the cages with our own hands, walked right in.

Daughter, she says. Stop letting your heart go hungry. This life doesn't need refining. It's most nourishing when plucked straight from the ground. Peel it with your teeth, lick the honey from the comb. Kiss wildly, surrender fully to the push and pull of the moon. You are your own ocean – vast and mysterious. Dive in. Swim naked in your depths. Love with abandon. Let yourself be taken. Be broken. Be opened. When the storm comes, welcome it in. Let the thunder roll through you, learn to strike when you need to. Your body will guide you – its intuition is the magic that dwells within.

Get sweaty. Get breathless.
Dance. Scream.
Live.

TO-DO LIST:

- Crack open the day, let it drip down your chin.
- Shake off the shackles, let loose your hair.
- When you inhale, let it fill your belly.
- When you feel, let it be with every inch of your skin.
- Drench yourself in sunlight.
- Bask in stillness.
- Let silence be the water you soak your bones in.
- Surrender to nature's calling – to the witchery of the trees,
- the dirt, the wind.
- If a storm comes, toss your head back, drink it in.
- Be present.
- Be wild.
- Be open.

YOU'RE SO ~~PRETTY~~ *UNRULY*

Look at you, you savage woman.
You, hair untamed, hands calloused woman.
You, go-ahead-and-pull-me-down woman.
You, *I'll just rise again, and again, and again.*
Look at your ~~thick~~ *full* belly that keeps you moving.
Look at your ~~flawed~~ *real* skin that tells your story.
Look at the love in your thighs, the way they
kiss each other.
Look at the fire in your eyes, with their
Medusa-stone power.
Turn around, look at the art you left in your wake.
The collection of beasts that stood in your way.
Monuments to the trouble you've made.

INSIDE JOB

I didn't leave the house today.
I put my lipstick on and did my hair and loved my body.
I opened the windows and let the wind touch my skin.
I drank bold, red wine and danced naked in the kitchen.
I basked in the sun and shivered at the warmth.
The earth is reclaiming me.
I am reclaiming me.
Today, I am seeking my breath.
It coats my lips and cheeks, and I want to inhale more
and exhale softer.
We make endless lists and check off the things we do,
but what do we really accomplish?
I burned my list this morning.
The remnants mix with the dirt on my feet.

"THERE IS NO REMEDY FOR LOVE BUT TO LOVE MORE"

— Henry David Thoreau

Tell me what pulls a shiver from your body.
What pricks the hair on the back of your neck,
your arms, your legs.
What makes your gut twist in that delicious way.
Tell me about your friends.
About the nights that turned into mornings.
About the dawn that kissed the darkened sky with her
pink-orange lips.
Tell me about your favorite indulgence.
What drink can you taste when it's mentioned.
What meal takes you home as soon as you inhale its delicious scent.
Tell me about the book you've read over and over.
The character you'll always long for.
The story you dream yourself into with every turn of a page.
Tell me what lights you on fire. What pulls you forward.
What shouts your name.
Tell me about the trip you can't wait to go on.
The shoreline you picture yourself walking.
The mountain you climb when you close your eyes.
Tell me about the song that transports you.
The one you have to dance to.
The one you turn to on those long, heavy drives.
Tell me how you've been broken open.
The bruises that make you human.
The wounds that taught you all the ways that love stays alive

STAY

I like it when you forget your keys.
The extra smile I get.
The extra kiss.
Can we spend a lifetime lingering by the door
never fully saying goodbye?

MY HUSBAND ASKS WHY I NEVER WRITE ABOUT HIM

Because you ruined me.
Tore my muse from my chest with your consistent presence,
your faithful hands.
How do I write about staying when you never leave?
How do I turn tears into diamonds when you
don't make me cry?
I can't speak of unsteady ground when I'm no longer shaking.
I can't lament one-sided affection when you've
balanced me out.

Love is now boring.
Unwavering.
Coffee in the morning, just how I like it.
The bed dipped and warm from the weight of your body
next to mine.

A head filled with flowers.
A kiss goodnight.

THE DIRT ALWAYS KNOWS

There is an ebb and flow in most things, isn't there?
A natural give and take.
Only so much energy exists. Only so much time.
I tell myself this on days like today when my mind and hands
are too full to empty themselves properly.
I collect, and collect, and collect until something gets dropped.
Lately, it's these moments of reflection. Of quiet contemplation.
Sleep is wakeful and even dreams are restless.
I am heavy and bloated and somehow empty and dissatisfied.
The weight I carry is not that of happiness, of days
brimming with joy.
It's more clutter than anything.
My body is always telling me things I do not want to know.
Change is coming, it whispers.
My joints hurt. My hips are stiff, and my shoulders carry a tension
I cannot ease.

This week I witnessed both life and death,
watched as a dying horse was released from her misery.
I cried as her companion feared her still-warm body.
Cried harder when his brave nose nudged hers, and his
muscles relaxed with understanding.
At the same moment my baby kicked in my belly.

Life and death.
Energy ever-shifting.

The mare's body now rests in the ground.
We walk above it. The grass grows again.
My baby is bigger every day.
More kicks. More restless life waiting for its time.
How many things do we put in the earth and how many
do we pull from it?

We forget and we remember. We lose and we gain.
The universe takes away something, but it's okay, the voices tell us,
something better will take its place.
I no longer believe in better.
I believe in different. I believe in change.

Life and death.
Energy ever-moving.

We forget and we remember.
We forget.
We forget.
We forget,
but the dirt always knows.

OLD FRIEND

I haven't lost you.
I whisper to my body in the morning
when my muscles are sore, and my joints are stiff.

I haven't lost you.
I pray as I open my palms
and soothe my stretching skin.

I haven't lost you.
My breasts swell and dip.

I haven't lost you.
My back arches and shifts.

I haven't lost you.
My belly changes color as it gives.

I haven't lost you. I haven't lost you. I haven't lost you.

We will find each other again.

A PROMISE

Your days won't always be perfect;
    the stars will align just to fall apart.
You will find love and you will lose it;
    you will question if it was even love at all.
You will realize that happiness is like the ocean,
    how it's deep and fickle and moves in waves,
and when it finally comes you will struggle to hold it,
only to watch with desperation as it escapes.

But with time you will learn
that no matter how often it leaves you,
it always comes back.

It always comes back.

YOU DON'T SAY *I LOVE YOU* OFTEN, BUT YOU SAY IT CONSTANTLY, QUIETLY, EVERY DAY

I think it first hit me when you said *we* instead of *me.*
It stuck when all the lights in ~~my~~ *our* house stopped going out.
When the remote control's battery never died,
when the fire alarm stopped randomly beeping.
On cold mornings, I go out to find my vehicle on,
hot air blasting, seat warmer already warm.
You make my coffee better than I do, cut my steak, peel my shrimp.
When we have fresh oysters, you set aside the best for me,
dress them up the way I like – lemon, spice, the rich saltwater
of the Gulf of Mexico tasting like your lips.
Sexy used to elude me even in high heels and a black dress,
but I feel sexy when you look at me
– hair unwashed, no bra, sweats,
lemon, spice, and saltwater dripping down my chin.
I laugh and say *it's because I'm the only option you have.*
You smile, but your eyes tell the whole story.
Later tonight, your hands will too.

SLOW LIVING

Early morning.
Coffee.
First light dances.
The dog trots over, licks my hand.
In the distance, your voice
calls me back to bed.

COMMON MIRACLES

after Khadijah Queen

A rooster greets the morning, and no matter where I am
in the world, I feel like I am home.

Your hands evoked the same feeling.
A sun rising. A new beginning. Possibility. Hope.

Sunflowers face each other when they can't find the light.
What's more beautiful than facing a storm together?
What's more meaningful than knowing there is someone
by your side?

Lightning struck the tree in my front yard during a storm.
It burst into flames before the rain smothered the burning.
Years later it is scarred and hollow but still thriving,
still so full of life.

I sit by myself, but I am not lonely.
There is the rooster, and the sunflowers, and the flourishing tree.
There is the morning, and the sun, and the memory
of your hands finding mine.

SALT

It was around 2:00pm when the collection of machines I was connected to stopped detecting my baby's heartbeat. My husband's eyes spoke the truth more than any of the nurses, and I did my best to pacify the storm rising in my chest.

Have you ever felt like you were drowning in your own body? Your mind the churning water and hope the distant surface? For the next few minutes, I was flipped around while cold hands moved gadgets across my belly, the soft thumps coming in waves before finally fading out.

I was at the bottom of the ocean when they cut me open.
Hearing my son's cry will always feel like taking my own
first breath.

The world is both beautiful and deadly, isn't it?
It can shock and awe. Destroy and mend. Burn and quench.
Our lives are coins just waiting to be flipped.

There is an ocean that now lives inside of me.
When I'm asked about another child, it rises in my mouth.
When I flick my tongue, I can taste the salt on my lips.

MATRESCENCE

I

What changes when you have a child?
Let me ask you this:
What remains the same?

II

The woman I used to be was cut out of me – I have the scar to prove it.
She let go easily, the wildness stronger than her innocence.
She closed her eyes one final time and opened the eyes of someone new.
She's harder. She's softer.
She's full, aching arms and untouched hair.
She's stretched and pulled and grasping.
She's scared and struggling to heal.
She's shed tears of love and exhaustion.
She's lost and finally seeing a glimpse of why she's here.

III

My mind is so full, yet so disjointed.
I feel a hundred different emotions at once.
How can you experience so much joy and suddenly be filled with more fear than ever before?
Mortality is tangible now.
My gut twists and my chest tightens at just the thought of losing what I've gained.
I dread my own mortality.
I dread the mortality of the life I brought into this world.
How could I breathe if I lost this?
How could I go on in darkness after experiencing this kind of light?
Each moment is precious.

Each laugh, and smile, and touch are a gift.
I want to hold on to each second.
I want to sit in this feeling of love until the end.

IV

I stand at the mirror and don't quite recognize the woman I see.
My feet are deeply rooted, yet I watch as parts of myself
slip away.
My hands are steady, yet I can feel my spirit shake.
How can you be so unsure of who you are
and suddenly see your purpose so clearly?
How can you be softer than you've ever been
and now have the courage to take on the world?
I'm not torn – I'm shifting.
I'm not something new – I'm just more than I was
yesterday.

THIS IS THE UNEDITED VERSION
THE COME DOWN

All tears.
All bite.
The night licks the salt from our cheeks, our cries ricochet.
We sway and crumble together.
We grasp not sure what we're looking to gain.
Isn't it beautiful? the world questions,
but there is only exhaustion.
It isn't inherent, what we're supposed to be feeling.
It isn't innate.
We're as raw as the life we are holding.
We're as fresh as the blood dripping down
our legs.

YOU HANDLE POSTPARTUM SO WELL

What you don't see are my husband's hands on my shoulders, his calming voice telling me he's happy to take over, the way he gently pulls my burdens into his arms.

What you don't hear is *don't worry about dinner, about*
the laundry, I'll clean up the house.

He tells me I'm beautiful, honors my new body,
gives it kindness when I can't.
He holds us both with the strength I'm not feeling,
brings peace when I'm shifting,
allows me to take, so I can give back.

SOFT, WHITE UNDERBELLY

Instead of allowing life to harden our bones,
we have to learn to soften.
I want to become breakable.
I want to become forgiving enough to grow.

I learned to worship the creature in me because I had to.
I had to love my body because it was the only thing that truly
belonged to me.

Walking the road of loneliness, I found the steady companion
that is my breath.
I found the ability to pardon myself while I struggled
to learn a language I was told to forget.

Self-love doesn't have to be a fickle wind that blows both
hot and cold.
Our truces don't have to be made unsteady when walking
unsteady ground.
We can hold ourselves as we crumble.
We can pardon each imperfect piece
we've found.

LOVER

The day is uncertain.
The sun did what she could to break through the grey sky,
but some seas are just too deep.
Still, the coffee is warm, and the wine is sweet.
Still, your hands are warm, and your lips are sweet.
Still, your shoes are beside mine by the door,
and our clothes hang together in the closet.
More constant than the grey sky.
More determined than the sun.

PRECIOUS

Some feelings have no words.
Some words are only a feeling,
sharp and deep, warm and spreading.
Your head falls to the side, eyes closed, lips slightly parted.
Sweet breath touches my face, and I tingle all over.
This is love, the silence whispers.
This is joy. This is hope.
What else is there but this moment?
What else is there but this life in my arms?
Precious, the silence whispers,
and I finally I understand.
The word.
The feeling.
Sharp and deep. Warm and spreading.

HOW MUCH DO I LOVE YOU?

I'll spend a lifetime cutting your food into bite-sized pieces.
I'll blow on each morsel, so you never burn your tongue.

WHAT LOVE WE HAVE LEFT

I hit an armadillo on the way to work. There was a split second I could see the fear in its eyes, its body frozen, its final moments the roar of an unkind world it was barely in.

That fear transferred itself into my belly, sunk like a rock. I swallow more pain every day, try to ignore the heaviness that is constantly growing, wonder if I can sew my lips shut without starving to death.

Later, I sit on the kitchen floor with my son eating yogurt mixed with chia seeds and strawberries. He dips his fingers into the sweet concoction, examines it closely before finally giving it a taste. With a second dip, he brings his fingers to my lips, smiles when I smile, laughs when I devour his tiny hand.

The waters rise, and I rise with them, hiding my face
so he doesn't see me cry.
He whines and reaches for me – he understands leaving,
but not coming back.

I want to live and not feel like I'm drowning.
I want to tell my son that there is good in this world, and it
not be a lie.

These days, I'm so full of rocks that the water keeps spilling.
The extent you feel pain, is the same extent you feel joy.

At this point, I must be an entire ocean.
Everywhere I go, I leak love.

MOTHERHOOD

I wasn't expecting the change.

I knew that life would be different – less sleep, less time,
less moments to breathe,
but there is a heaviness now that wasn't there before.

Life is short, isn't it?
Moments are fleeting, aren't they?

Happiness and peace are fragile things that I now hold
with careful hands.
Storms can form in clear-blue skies and bright days still end
in darkness.
I enjoy the sun now more than ever. I bask in the finiteness of the day.

Life is precious, isn't it?
Moments are gifts, aren't they?

EMPTY

We've all been told about the finiteness of storms.
The sun after the clouds.
The fresh smell that follows.
It will settle, they say.
The dust or the rain or the pain
you've been carrying.
You'll learn how to put it down.
If that's true, then why are my hands empty
and my back still hurting?
Why are the clouds continuously swirling
and the sun still blocked from view?
I'm trying desperately to love this world,
but the truth is, it's as ugly as it is beautiful,
and much of the ugliness is found on the edge of a human's hands,
on the tip of a human's tongue.
And let us not forget what it truly means to be human.
Somewhere along the line we started to confuse power with existence.
We dug wells so deep that they can never be full.

Maybe the storms are of our own making.
Maybe we create the pain because it's better than feeling
nothing at all.

I'M SORRY IF WE DON'T LEAVE YOU ANYTHING WORTH HAVING

Someone sends me a video of a father cradling an infant.
The body still, the cries silenced.
The father, wailing. Pacing. Clutching.
A head rolls back, vacant eyes meet his.

My pain doesn't matter, so I won't speak of it.
The sky rains fire, but here it is quiet.
I hold my son in much the same way,
feel the rise and fall of his chest,
steady as the waves that seem endless.
What type of destruction could stop their movement?
How devastating a thing to witness.

Art is supposed to be as beautiful as it is honest,
but how do you turn anger into a blossoming flower?
How do you write anguish into a sunset,
promise that after this darkness, the light will come again?
How do you find hope in a breath that ends?

My son shifts in my arms, head rolls back, bright eyes meet mine.
I can't write of beauty, so I'll try honesty instead.
Death isn't a vulture circling in some distant future.
It walks. It stands.
It feels the same fears.
It has the same hands.

How devastating a thing to witness.
Something so beautiful can turn so ugly in the end.

I WOULD SAY THAT I WISH OUR CURRENCY WAS FLOWERS, BUT ALL I CAN PICTURE ARE FIELDS OF DAISIES RIPPED OFF AT THE STEM

The other day, I watched a person swerve to hit an animal
trying to cross the road, another opens his window
to toss garbage into the street.
Is this what God pictured when he started his greatest work?
What are we if not caricatures of ourselves?
Most days, I find it all heavy and not at all funny,
so I walk among the trees when I need to remember the beauty.
Humanity seems so dark most days that even the sun shining down
can't bring us to the light.
Cold, closed hands and hardened jaws.
Eyes so focused that the world is blurred.
Mouths so open that we only hear our own screaming.
But to close our mouths and listen?
But to close our eyes and finally see?
Isn't that what the wind is for?
Just a feeling.
Isn't that what the trees do?
Quietly absorb the light.

ISN'T EVERY DAY THE END OF THE WORLD FOR SOMEONE?

The air smells like lighting. My heart is a thunderclap.
Some days come at you like a wave.
Some days are just for the anger, for the rain.
I stand on the edge and swallow the swell.
I clench my fists and hold back the crashing in my throat.
The truth is
some days are already sinking.
The truth is
the sun rising doesn't always feel like hope.

ON THE DAYS YOU FEEL LESS THAN

Remember that we are all on a spinning rock shooting
through darkness.
Which is ridiculous.
Which is magic.
Which makes your life nothing short of a miracle, your breath
as incredible as the sun.

On the days you're placing your entire existence in the cons' column,
remember that you're comparing your bad to
everyone else's good.
That the pictures you see are of filtered smiles, touched up eyes.
That humans are incredible liars.

On the days you're tired of the world,
remember that there is never a shortage of captivating,
unbelievable things.
Bees dance to give directions.
Butterflies taste with their feet.
At daybreak it's actually the bird song that awakens the trees.

“I’M EGGSHELL FINE: CURRENTLY WHOLE BUT EASILY CRUSHED”

So I count my reasons, each smidgin of joy a new link of armor in my
thinning skin.
Every morning a wren sits in the center of our front door wreath
and sings his heart out.
Our satsuma tree is covered in blossoms, its branches
humming with life as bees drunkenly sway from
flower to flower, their pollen-saddled legs slowing them down.
Yesterday, we jumped from crescent to crescent, the eclipse
casting celestial shadows across the ground.
You were an asteroid, I a forgotten moon.
Last night, I dreamt of floating in darkness.
This morning, the exhale of the night greets me,
warm and damp.

LOVE IS COMPLICATED

But has someone reached for your hand, and you responded
without thinking?
Intertwined your fingers with theirs, stepped into the storm.

Yesterday evening I watched a finch settle atop her chicks,
understood the look of calm that washed across her body,
the sudden softness in her eyes.
I sipped on the wine my lover poured for me,
inhaled deeply to pull the smell of his shirt into my body,
smiled at the roar of his laughter coming from inside.
Later that night, my mother called. She needed me in the morning.
Of course, I'll be there.
As simple as breathing.
As innate as the sun breaking through the night,
unspoken but consistent,
subtle but bright.

A STRANGER ON THE STREET RETURNS A SMILE,

and I am reminded of the light filtering through the trees in the morning, the bright purple-pink of evening, the way the stars shine when the clouds clear. I think of the moon peeking through my window, the soft, warm breath of a dog curled beside me, the smell of coffee drifting through the air. I can hear the unfiltered joy of a child's laughter, the subtle song of wind chimes dancing, ocean waves crashing, wild birds greeting the dawn. I can see the delicate lines around the eyes of my best friend when she's happy, feel a lover's sigh of satisfaction, smell the earth's response to summer's sun.

There is beauty everywhere, isn't there?
Tenderness woven into each moment.
Kindness waiting to be noticed.
Peace begging to be found.

DOLCE FAR NIENTE
SWEET IDLENESS

We talk about the future, always the future.
Rain in the forecast, the grocery list,
family is coming to town this weekend,
the yard needs to be mowed,
the house needs to be cleaned, and the dishes,
why are there always fresh dishes in the sink?
When was the last time we turned off auto-pilot,
settled into our senses,
focused on something other than the next thing we have to do,
the next place we have to be?

Let's stop carving out our bodies to move faster.
Let's rest long enough for the fog to lift.

Right now, the light is hitting the window perfectly making little rainbows shimmer across the floor. Dinner is sizzling – dill, shallots, and lime. There is the *pop* of beer cans opening, the rustle of tree limbs as the evening wind starts its nightly dance. The dog trots over, her soft tongue-lick grazes my hand.

Let's not devour this moment; I want to
consume it slowly.
Let our lips taste each salty drop as they roll past.

The future will come when it's ready.
If we get there first, what is there to do anyway
but look back?

I WANT TO STAY YOUNG FOREVER

My son just noticed the moon for the first time.
He points at it with his chubby fingers and looks back at me
to make sure I see it too.
It's the white-yellow of a zested lemon and nearly full.
Around us, the trees are dancing, the air is warm and smells of
tea olive and mud.
Our newest residents settle above us.
Vultures, high in the pines, their wings sweeping like
black paint brushes marking the orange sky.

He is rapt and my heart is as full as the moon.
I want to stay this young forever,
  – not in age, but in wonder.
I want to burn with the curiosity that I see in his eyes.
I want him to look at me and know that this fire doesn't have to die.
That joy is as boundless as a bird painting the heavens.
That hope is as light and abundant as the feathers gracing
its wings.

NEWBORN

I'm reborn.
My eyes look on with the grey-blue of something untouched
by the light.
My heart sees with the bright optimism of something untouched
by the dark.
My skin smells of daybreak – dew-tipped grass, dirt, and sun.
My blood once again pumps with purpose, and my hands know
only tenderness,
my chest, comfort,
my thoughts, hope.
This ancient world is suddenly a fresh, wide wonder.
Flowers, brighter.
Trees, wiser.
The sky, endless.
I no longer dream of flying with the birds,
I soar with them.
I no longer shy from the wind,
I squeal as it dances across my skin.
What a sensation, this living.
What a gift, this seeing the world as beautiful
again.

MOTHER

The world is a death trap,
but have you noticed her beauty?
Even with her snarling lips,
even with her snapping jaws.
Those lips contain a tongue that licks new life
until eyes are open.
Those teeth gently carry young.
Isn't everything about creation and destruction?
Aren't we all born and spend a lifetime slowly dying?
Haven't we all wrapped our fingers around someone's throat
and called it love?
Not everyone's been licked, but we all dream of dripping warmth,
of tender teeth.
Most days I don't believe in a higher power,
but today I am sitting alone in a field and something
is speaking to me.
It might be the trees – they are buzzing with pulsing, hot life
and their leaves are making love to the wind.
I lay back and feel the ground beating.
Her mouth wraps around my body
and holds me close.

ALL OF THESE ARE TRUE

I make good money. I make less money than my closest friends, and ~~some~~ *most* days it bothers me. I have a small army on social media, but no bestsellers. My last royalty payment for my second book was just over two hundred dollars. The last direct message thanking me for my work was only moments ago.

Recently, I joined a group of women on a bachelorette party and felt inadequate because of my small (*real*) eyelashes, my thin (*real*) hair, and my belly that changed with the birth of my son. The same belly he likes to cuddle into, his safe space, his first home.

I pride myself on having my shit together. I work full time, manage a business on the side, am a daughter, a friend, a mother, a wife. Yesterday, I locked my keys in my car with my child inside. Later, I opened the wrong tab on the salt n' pepper shaker and ruined dinner with one flick of my wrist. Afterward, I drank too much wine and cried in the shower, my new false lashes sliding down my face.

This morning, I woke up smiling, rolled over and
started writing.
What a relief to know how perfectly human I am.

PUT YOUR OWN OXYGEN MASK ON FIRST

Take that bath. That day off. That long pause. Buy the outfit that makes you feel good. The oils for your skin. The lipstick someone told you was too bold for your lips. Allow yourself to feel beautiful. To feel wanted. To feel loved. Disconnect from your expectations. Turn off autopilot. Remove the bandages. Let your wounds heal in the sun. Learn the meaning of *silience*. Take notice. Take care. Take walks. Break out the good wine. The dark chocolate. The art that sits half-done. Sit in the cool air of an early morning. In the healing salt of the ocean. In the quiet of a moment you finally took for yourself.

Cry when you need to. Scream if it helps you.
Close your eyes. Exhale.
Succumb.

ESPECIALLY WHEN

Even when you feel like a million scattered pieces,
you are still whole.
Even when you're unsure of the path you're walking,
you still have purpose.
Even when your lover leaves you empty and begging,
you are still loved.
Even when you've tried and tried and failed and failed,
you are still worthy.
Even when,
especially when.

"THE LONGER I LIVE THE MORE BEAUTIFUL LIFE BECOMES"

— Frank Lloyd Wright

I used to show my body off,
but now I try to hide it.
A good morning is one where I pull on my underwear,
and I don't pinch the fat on my stomach and sigh.
Vultures now nest in the trees around my house.
I can hear their wings as they wake,
hear the branches bend and creak as they depart for the day.
I'm smiling, but I'm holding my breath.
Who would have thought that suffocation
could look so beautiful, could be so easy?
It's difficult when the news says that we are all fucked,
that the world is crumbling,
that the earth has tired bones and is trying to
unburden herself.
Life is pretty ugly much of the time,
and humans are pretty shitty, especially to each other.

Still, we don't have to wait to be betrayed by our failings.
Still, we don't have to label mistakes as failings at all.

Still, the wind says *listen. listen. listen.*
Still, the trees roar with one voice.
Still, the sun splashes over skin with warming fingers.
Still, I think there is a lesson in this morning light.

Self-pity might not kill you, but it will kill the joy
before you can feel it.
It will pull clouds across the sun,
suck the color from the sky, the eyes of a stranger,
the lips of a potential lover you'll never let close enough
to touch.

It isn't really delicate, this life.
Soft, yes. It bruises easy.
Difficult, yes. We all carry the weight.

Still, the orange tree continues to blossom.
Still, the sticky juices run down my arm as I
lick my fingers.
Still, they're as sweet as the previous year.

AN ANTHEM FOR MY C-SECTION SCAR AFTER CHILDBIRTH

after Kara Jackson

The first time my husband saw my ravaged, naked body, he quipped how it now looked like I was always smiling. My boobs were two round eyes, my belly button a tiny nose, my new red-rimmed, raised incision the thin, upturned lips.

It's an image I can't unsee.

Now, when I'm on the brink of self-loathing, when I feel like the mess on the floor that no one wants to clean, I run my fingers over the tender, blooming flesh and remember how happily it opened, how being ripped is sometimes the only way love can expand.

I'LL STOP WRITING ABOUT LOVING MY BODY WHEN I'VE FINALLY LEARNED TO LOVE MY BODY

Until then, when I want to grab my stomach and squeeze,
I will embrace it instead.
When *I love you* tastes bitter and polished, I will close my eyes
and think of my life,
how the *extra* is just the remnants of joy left behind.
When the years speak through the stiffness in my shoulders,
I will draw a bath and soak my aching limbs, my working spine.
I will bow my head at the burdens they carry,
how gracefully they move when the day gets weighty,
how willing they are to keep going despite the heaviness of life.
I will rub oil into my skin, run a delicate finger over
each stretch, each divot, each line.
I will thank her for always staying with me,
for her forgiveness,
for never holding resentment when I allow the world
to tell me what love should look like.

I WON'T CALL YOU PRETTY

You are the piercing scream of a banshee. The haunting melody of a siren's song. As tempting as you are terrifying. As powerful as you are soft. You are lightning on a clear afternoon – surprising and exhilarating, penetrating and sharp. A spark that pricks each nerve ending. A roar you can feel in your gut. Your smile is a torch in the darkest tunnel. Your laughter is the sun.

You are salt spray on a wound that needs healing. The first gulp of air
after sinking. The first sip of water after days of merciless heat.

As unwavering as the light of morning.
As stirring as a storm approaching.
As unbridled as the sea.

JOY HARJO SAID, "THE HEART IS THE SMALLER COUSIN OF THE SUN",

and I feel its warmth already.
Each beat is a ray reaching for my extremities.
I am a tiny world of jungle and water, and the endless heat
is creating all this humidity.
How can I keep myself from crying when this water
needs to be released?
How can I not feel when there is a bird of paradise blooming
in my chest,
a howler monkey calling in my throat,
a panther creeping along my collarbone
just waiting for her moment.
My head is the moon and accepting this has led me closer to the truth.
Aren't we all just reflections of ourselves?
Shadows and shimmers of our honest needs,
our candid wants.
I look to the pool collecting in my belly, finally unafraid
of what I might find.
Something wild, surely.
Isn't savage just another word
for free?
Yes, something savage.
Something free.

"LOVE YOURSELF. THEN FORGET IT. THEN LOVE THE WORLD."

— Mary Oliver

I think I've finally learned to love myself;
at least, it is suddenly and sharply
no longer important.
I've realized my insignificance, and it is freeing.
How powerful it is to know that I am nothing more
than what I am now, in this moment.
Eyes and heart and wonder observing birds dancing
in a field of glistening light,
      drinking from water droplets,
            singing to the sun as she greets the sky.
It is morning and life is waking inside and around me.
What more is there beyond bearing witness
to such quiet beauty?
What purpose could I serve beyond the breath
catching in my throat?

THE THING ABOUT TRAGEDY

It's not a tidal wave – *that you can see coming,*
but it drowns you just the same.

THE BEST OF YOU

The bleeding never started.
There was no discomfort, no sign, no cramping.
My body still lush and expecting.
My belly still grasping lovingly to what little was left.

I don't think I'll ever forget the sight of the blackhole staring back at me.
I don't think I'll ever understand how something can exist and then not.
A heartbeat vanished. A tiny body nowhere to be found.

They say it's not uncommon.
They say these things happen.
They say you can always try again,

a life taken can simply be replaced.

Before I was drowning in an ocean, but now I'm on an island.
Alone and burning.
Drained, but full of something I'll never fully release.

Yesterday they scraped me clean, but I don't feel empty.
I know I still carry the best of you in me.

INVISIBLE WORK

I squeeze my hands waiting for stone to turn into diamond,
but all I'm left with are sore hands and a pile of dust
at my feet.
Maybe not everything can be changed into something precious.
Maybe it is precious, but not what I need.
I don't want another way to survive.
I don't want steadier shoulders and stronger legs,
there isn't a burden I can't carry.
Still, how do I process this grief?
We sit across from each other silently.
Eyes unwavering. Breath in sync.
We are one in the same, aren't we?
Both stone trying to be diamond.
Both precious as we are, but not what
we want to be.

"YOU DON'T ALWAYS HAVE TO BE GRACEFUL"

— Anne Hathaway

Or put together. Or ready. Or assured.
Your scream doesn't have to be soundless.
You don't have to be all heart and no break.

You can rise like the rooster in the morning:
face skyward, mouth open, full-bellied rage.

A READER ROLLS HER EYES, WONDERS WHY I ASK IF PEOPLE ARE STRUGGLING, SAYS HER LIFE IS PERFECT AND PEOPLE ARE FINE

Meanwhile, I exchange stories with a woman who just
had a miscarriage, tell her about the one I had a few months ago.
We discuss how comforting it is to know that we have each other,
how there is a bit of peace restored in realizing that you aren't alone.
Another recently discovered that she has breast cancer
– surgery completed and chemo to come.
She's trying to wrap her head around it, doing what she can
to stay strong.
Another's mother is dying. She tells me how close they are,
how devastated she is.
I say, *I'm sorry*, but what are words when you're losing your
best friend.

There is loneliness, isolation, anxiety, and depression.
Cheating, divorce, and trying despite the ache.
Work that is draining.
Burnout because *who can afford to take a few days?*

A handful just want to look in the mirror and like
their reflection.
Some just want to feel accepted.
Others just want to feel loved.
All just want a connection, that nod of understanding,
that light in the dark.

"HOW CAN I BEGIN ANYTHING NEW WITH ALL OF YESTERDAY IN ME?"

— Leonard Cohen

Each day is a new one, but how do I let go of the baggage
I carried to bed?
How do I toss it into the night if it's the only thing
that keeps me company when the darkness stretches herself
across my body?
When I become more stomach than heart.
When the truth buries itself behind my smile,
and I can't dig it out.
Once the light fades, the things I could not speak start screaming.
My mind turns into a hall of mirrors,
and I am haunted by my face over, and over, and over again.
Are we even solid creatures without the heaviness of grief?
Can beauty come from things that are not at all beautiful?
Can we both bleed and sing?

Tonight, I can continue this bloodletting,
or I can move beyond the shelter of my body and greet the storm.
Maybe the earth is simply calling to her lover.
I think about her feral heart.
I think I will no longer be afraid of the ache in mine.
Brave is the heart that beats with abandon.
Brave is the heart that bleeds and sings.
One day I'll be able to speak into the light,
and the night will not scare me.
I'll join her as one of her creatures – savage like the earth's
pounding heart.
I will become the lover she beckons to.
What are we if not blood and song?

YOU CREATE YOUR LIFE AS YOU MOVE

Isn't the morning the heaviest just before the sun rises?
I know, I know,
who wants to hear day by day and step by step
when the days and the steps feel endless.
What kind of advice is *keep going* when the pink horizon
is always just out of reach.
When the mountain stretches before you and disappears
into the sky.
When that sky looks to be more mist than stars
from where you're standing.

Still, you create your life as you move.

And if you make it to the top of the mountain, what then?
What will you do when you hover like the mist – wet and cold?
When it's not what you dreamed the peak would be – just you
and the sky.
It's a beautiful thought, limitless air, and clarity,
but the truth is, we all obscure our own view.

Still, you create your life as you move.

Aren't we all just tiny birds clutched in the palm
of the world?
I've seen the wind snap pines in two and topple oaks
regardless of their thick trunks and reaching branches.
There is always something stronger.
Always something that can snap and topple you.

Still, you create your life as you move.

There is no such thing as ready,
and *should be* is a dangerous rut to fall into.
Haven't we all dreamed our lives with child eyes?

And even after we've crumpled these dreams and tossed them
in the corner of our hearts,
don't we still unfold and read them again and again?

Still, you create your life as you move.

We all want a keyhole to look through.
Something just large enough to see if there is happiness
on the other side.
Do you want to know a secret?
All doors block darkness, and all futures carry no light;
your story comes with you when you walk through.

You create your life as you move.

BREAK AND MAKE IT BEAUTIFUL

Leonard Cohen said,
"There is a crack in everything, that's how the light gets in,"
but I feel like mine is escaping.
Maybe I am more shatter than crack.
More split open and gaping than ripped and stitched.
Some days I'm drowning in myself and today the water is high.
Tomorrow's breath is already heavy, and my heart is
pounding in my head.
The rhythm I typically move to is now bringing me
to my knees.
I do not know silence.
My mind is too much a stubborn ass to stop her braying.
My shoulders tremble as I try to trap the pain in my chest.
I open my mouth for release, but my body holds too tightly –
 even after all this time, I still have not learned how to let go.
I look to the moon who sits dimly in the sky,
half-shrouded in darkness.
Break, it whispers. *Break and make it beautiful.*

WHATEVER IT TAKES

Not all worlds can be made anew,
but there isn't a world that can't be loved
in new ways.
My mind doesn't want forgiveness,
but I'll still stand here and give it.
My body doesn't feel deserving of worship,
but I'll wrap my arms around it anyway.
I made a promise to search for my worth even when
I can't see it.
I made a promise to swallow the fear even if I have to break it off
piece by piece.

There is always light even when I'm swimming in darkness.
I will become that light even when the darkness is me.

I KNOW I AM A MOTHER

I stand in the bathroom.
My husband beckons. Calls me sexy.
Reminds me that the kids are asleep
and the night is ours.

I know I am a mother.
I've learned how the growl becomes instinctual,
how tears in the shower keep me from breaking,
how *tender* is actually a verb.
I know that tomorrow's tasks are already written,
that days happen in an instant,
that exhaustion makes it easy to turn my back
on who I once was.

I know I am a mother,
but am I still a woman?
Where is the confident strut,
the supple, tempting skin,
the laughing eyes?

I want to feed her and hold her and allow her to cry.
I will not berate her for being hungry, for longing,
for letting go as she became something new –

– I will mother her too.

THE STATE OF YOUR HOUSE IS THE STATE OF YOUR MIND

Mine is cluttered with toddler toys and to-do lists. The floor needs to be swept and there are dishes in the sink. Around every corner, you'll find another half-finished project, another item waiting to be put back, another dark-stained glass holding long-cold coffee.

Some days the paint-chipped walls complain about the weight of the day, but the bones are always steady. In the evenings, the light through the windows is soft and warm, a cattail palm growing in the dusty-yellow rays, an unfinished book dog-eared and waiting.

The kitchen is full of food and laughter, and the refrigerator is covered in more pictures than reminders. In the living room my son's joy echoes as the dog licks his fingers. Down the hall you'll find the unmade bed where my lover calls to me.

MY SON BRINGS ME THINGS THAT HE FINDS INTERESTING

A leaf, dried and cracked.
Some grass he's pulled from the ground,
roots still attached, dirt swinging.
A flower with only one petal, the others crushed crimson in his palm.
He points to a lizard, a rotting log, a pair of vultures
circling overhead.
He rolls in the grass with the family dog, unabashedly learning
her pleasures.
He follows her into alcoves, bushes grown over,
sacred, hidden places you have to dream of to find.
He chatters, nonsensical to those who listen too closely,
a primordial language, to the crows watching nearby.

As the sun dips, he hands me a sprig of clover.
I don't need to count the leaves to know how lucky it is.

THE CLOSER YOU STEP TO THE EDGE, THE MORE BEAUTIFUL THE VIEW

The days drag. The nights do too when you're too tired to sleep. But the weeks, the weeks seem to slip away in a single ragged breath. Are we ever one word? One definition? I'm not sure that I've ever felt truly content. Happy, yes. Joyous, on occasion, but were the moments ever enough to fully exhale? I can feel the next breath building while I let go of the last, a new shape forming as the one before finds itself.

The surest way to lose your voice is to use someone else's, but how do you find your own when it seems like every word has already been spoken? When the noise is deafening, and silence is the one thing you crave? Ghosts are wishes long forgotten, and we are all haunted by the dreams we forgot to chase.

I've grown tired of pining for something I can't name, so I think I'll turn my eyes outward. The sun is a warmer mistress than my thoughts, and the grass is a softer bed. If I've learned anything, it's this: If you want to find magic, you have to believe in it. If you want forgiveness, you have to give it.

So, forgive yourself as you leave the desert and step into the pool that is your body. Forgive yourself as you slip into the cool after years of unrelenting heat. There is magic in missteps and miscalculations. There is beauty in accepting life for all that it can be.

COME AS YOU ARE

My body asks:

Should I hide the new swell of my thighs?
And what about these dimples, these rolls,
these skin-stretched lines?
I used to be as smooth as a lake in the morning,
as fresh as the light that dances on the surface.

Have you noticed the years collecting around
my throat, my eyes?
Weren't my breasts once fuller, my waist more defined?
And my lips, no longer plump and tempting, my mouth no longer
gentle enough to kiss.

Am I firm enough to be desired?
Am I soft enough to be grasped?

I run my fingers over her expanse,
feel the warmth of her flesh.

Come as you are, I tell her.
You're perfect as is.

I LOVE MY BODY

I pamper my body because it makes her feel beautiful.
I do her hair, and oil her skin, and paint her lips.

I indulge my body because it makes her feel abundant.
Blueberries from the vine, dark chocolate, deep, red wine.

I honor my body because it makes her feel cherished.
Hold her close. Remind her how vital she is.

I respect my body because she deserves to *flourish.*

THE GREATEST GIFT I CAN GIVE MY DAUGHTER

To love myself so loudly that when someone tells her
that she looks just like her mother, there is no question how
beautiful I think she is.

To accept myself so wholly that there is no *soon, after, when*
I gain/lose/change.
There is only now. Skin exposed to the kiss of sunshine,
body free of restrictions, belly fed.

To not dwell on what the magazines call imperfections.
Unkempt and untouched.
Wrinkles. Sags. Stretches. Lines.
Who cares, aging is a fact of life.

To embrace my body *as is, as is, as is.*

HAPPINESS

Happiness is a few pounds heavier.
It's accepting being tired.
Being older. Being softer.
Being more reaching oak and less wildflower.
Happiness is taking days to bask in silence.
Not doing. Just being.
Happiness is no longer shrinking.
It's releasing.
    Guilt. Regret.
The weight of the past, and the fear of the future.
It's discovering the joy in simplicity.
The beauty in the little things.
The power in the everyday.

ADULTING *(IT'S CALLED BALANCE, DARLING)*

Just moments ago, an ant bit my toe, and I resisted the urge to press it between my thumb and finger. Earlier, I illustrated the same restraint when I rewrote an email five times before finally hitting send. I have fifteen unread voicemails on my personal phone. I don't even know what the passcode to my work phone is. I run meetings, make decisions, but when I go grocery shopping, I forget things that are written on my list.

Somedays, I work out for an hour, carry around a jug of water,
make sure to get all of my steps in.
Somedays, self-care is dinner in a bag and the TV entertaining
the kids.

Most mornings, I rise tired, try to love my body
with expensive creams and gentle hands,
try to hide the negative self-talk with sappy affirmations.
Most evenings, I go to bed flipping through picture after picture
of filtered bodies, wondering if Botox would fix my smile lines,
my drooping lids.

Tomorrow, I'll wake up to a sink full of dishes.
Tonight, I'm finishing a $7 bottle of wine and sleeping
with my husband instead.

CHAOTIC GOOD

We are potty training, and my son just discovered the joy of no pants.
Unencumbered, he runs faster.
Jumps. Rolls. Climbs.
There are clothes left in his wake, dribbles of urine scattered
across the floor.
We rejoice in the little wins – making it to the bathroom,
controlling the spray.
He dances with each success, expects everyone to celebrate.

He's learning life, and I'm learning patience.
How to slow down, laugh at the mistakes.

Let the air entice you.
Toss off all constraints.

SILIENCE

I don't want clutter. *Things*.
I want shadows dancing on the porch. A soft breeze.
Laughter echoing from the yard. My breath, a practiced art.

I want to feel the ricochet of rain drops through open windows.
Let the thunder move through me until my skin feels like a spark.

I want books just for entertainment.
Wild romances. Thrillers. Poetry.
Beauty for the sake of beauty. Art for the sake of art.

I want my eyes to flutter open in the mornings, *slowly*.
I want to kiss you like a flower opening, *slowly*.
I want to notice the intricacies – ants on a railing,
the veins of a leaf,
the way your lips part when you're looking at me.

I WILL SWALLOW THE SUN

Another year, and I am grateful.

My busy mind plays this game where I imagine
that I can no longer feel the morning air
or smell the honeysuckle that grows wild
at my mother's house.
I can no longer hear the birds.
No longer touch my husband's hands or feel my son's head
on my chest.
I imagine myself opening as wide as possible and swallowing
them whole.
I wrap them in my skin. Marry them to my bones.
Promise to myself that even death cannot separate us.
Death.
The world is spinning and falling as it shoots through darkness.
This I understand.
Spinning. Falling. Darkness.
These are tangible things every human has touched.
But Death?
It takes light to create shadows,
and I am now so full of light that I see shadows everywhere.

Another year, and I am grateful.

Today, I can feel the morning air, and smell the honeysuckle,
and hold my husband's hands.
Today, my son rests in my arms, and I can focus on his breath.
Still, time is trying to turn into a series of tasks, a list of chores
I didn't make it to.
    Tomorrow. Tomorrow they will get done.
You can find sustenance in the muck of it all, I remind myself.
Nutrients come from the sighs, the tears, the laughter, the moans.
Your hands are busy working even if you don't realize it,
I remind myself.

Yes, tomorrow.
Tomorrow they will get done.
Today,
today I will swallow the sun.

"AGING IS AN EXTRAORDINARY PROCESS WHERE YOU BECOME THE PERSON YOU ALWAYS SHOULD HAVE BEEN."

— *David Bowie*

Where you finally learn the weight of a moment,
the importance of laughter,
the value of taking a day to yourself.
Where intimacy becomes less about the breathless moments
and more about the people who help
you catch your breath.
Where you can finally stretch your limbs,
kick out the sides of the box you put yourself in.
Where you might feel like you've lost the glamor,
but dammit if your confidence isn't sexier,
your aura more alluring, your quiet grace more enticing
than that shimmering fountain of youth.

Where your heart is now your armor and not the sword
that pierces you through.

Where you can let go of the pretenses, the ego,
the unsteady ground.
Where you don't need to be anyone other than
who you are now.

HOME

My hair is turning grey, and my stomach has the look of someone
who eats okay and doesn't sleep well.
My back aches from the weight of existing,
and my hands are sore from holding it all together.
I ~~walk~~ *dance* in the middle-ground of life.
Not yet old. No longer young.

And Lord, am I beautiful.
And Lord, am I full.

My husband grasps my curves and calls me sexy.
My son clings to my neck and calls me home.

YOU CAN KEEP YOUR SAPLING BODY

I want to be a mountain.
Live oak limbs and black gum roots.

I want a base, ample and unshakeable.
Thick and steady. Storm-ready.
Resolute.

I want skin intimate with the wind, the sun, the rain.
Weathered enough to tell stories. A testament to my strength.

I want bones trained to carry.
Veins that flow like rivers to my ocean of
a heart.

You can keep your *pre*.
You can keep your *new*.

I want after.
I want profuse.

A NEW KIND OF SEXY

Hair wild kind of sexy.
Hands full kind of sexy.
Good food and strong wine kind of sexy.
Crow's feet and smile lines kind of sexy.
Age is just a number kind of sexy.
Dog-tired but still dancing kind of sexy.
Beat-down but still singing kind of sexy.
I know what I want kind of sexy.
I know who I am kind of sexy.
The kind of sexy that says
this life is well-lived.

I WOKE UP TODAY

I've found my joy,
and oh what a feeling,
and oh what a realization that it was there all along.
Eyes see clearer after a storm has passed,
and the clouds are finally moving.
When was the last time you noticed your breath as you took it?
I inhale deeply and rejoice in the swell of my lungs.
Love says, you don't need to be more than you are at this moment,
and I finally believe it.
Love says, here, take my hand,
and I do.
Love says, I'll be with you in the morning,
and together we prepare to greet the sun.

IF YOU'RE ALIVE, THEN ACT ALIVE

The human heart beats approximately 100,000 times a day
    – give it a reason to beat faster.
The human body has trillions of nerve endings
    – give them something to feel.
You're going to break, so let it be wide open.
You're going to fumble, so let it be towards something worth crawling to.

That thing that calls your name, chase it.
That thing that rattles your bones, do it until your courage drowns out the fear.
When your soul growls, feed it.
When your skin tugs, shapeshift into something new.

Your life is bread. Eat it. Soak it in salted butter, in rich olive oil and deep vinaigrette.
Slurp the day – *mouth open, belly ready,*
let the remnants stain your lips.

Dance, your steps don't have to be rhythmic.
Sing, who cares if you can't.
Write postcards to who you once were.
Let them see how well you lived.

"ALL GOOD THINGS ARE WILD AND FREE"

— Henry David Thoreau

for Evan

I want your fingers stained purple from picking the blueberries
your grandfather planted.
I want your toes dirty and damp from running barefoot
in the early morning grass.
I want laughter to be your companion, tears to be the cousin
you welcome but don't visit often,
curiosity to be the friend you always keep close at hand.

I want your neck and shoulders sun-kissed from days
spent in wonder,
your heart as strong as the limbs that carry you to the edge.
I want a soul like water – powerful and bending and
constantly seeking.
I want strength through softness, power through kindness,
open hands.

I want a spirit unburdened by the nightfall that finds us all
in the end.

PREGNANCY AFTER MISCARRIAGE

We tread lightly, speak softly,
this gift is glass, and we already know how easily it can
break.

A WOMAN ON INSTAGRAM SAYS SHE CAN HELP ME STAY SMALL WHILE PREGNANT

And I think of cells splitting,
the earth erupting, molten life bubbling and mounting,
creating as she moves.
I think of blossoms unfolding,
fruit in the sun, split and bursting, seeds spewing,
succulent flesh exposed and begging
to be consumed.
I think of wisteria in the spring, lilac-covered and spreading,
butterflies nectar-drunk and dancing,
bees heavy and swaying with their harvest clinging to
their legs.

I think of storms too full to hold themselves together,
trees too lush to not spill onto the ground.

I think of the universe in my belly, kicking and expanding,
fighting
to be anything but
small.

WOMAN MIGHT BE A SCIENCE, BUT IT'S ALSO AN ART

For my daughter

You are new, but you house something ancient.
A woman's energy never dies, it moves.

The world is aching, and you will ache with it.
A woman's strength is in her ability to burn and still live.

When you feel that yearning, don't try to control it.
A woman's spirit is meant to be an unbridled tempest.

When you're lost, reach for your sisters.
A woman's love is as nourishing and abundant as roots.

When you're older, you will start bleeding.
A woman's body is an open wound.

FERAL HOUSEWIFE

She'll stay home, raise the children, but don't always expect
dinner on the table and your house to be clean.
She's outside, feet bare, giving what she can give
and taking what she needs.
All broken edges and dancing light,
she doesn't judge the curves of her body;
she already knows every inch is a journey,
her worth a pool of water in this merciless heat.
She's teaching her daughter about reclaiming, rebellion,
and paths untaken.
She's showing her son that *the way it's always been* doesn't mean
it's the way it should be.
Her heart beats with all four chambers;
she breathes with both lungs.
She isn't trained.
She isn't tame.
She's free.

THIS IS GOING TO BE AN ORDINARY LIFE

One with sunsets and sunrises, early mornings with sleep stuck in your eyes, late nights where weariness wraps her arms around you and holds you so close that you can barely breathe. One where the trip to work is long, the work is long, and your heart is mostly elsewhere. You will spend hours making the same mess of yourself over and over, cleaning up that mess again and again. Age won't come fast enough until it suddenly comes too quickly. Coffee or wine or cigarettes will become a crutch. Friends will come and go. Lovers will leave their marks. Your heart will sway between bursting and empty, between shattered and pristine.

You will fall in love; it probably won't be the love you imagined as a child – less rush and more steady, less thrill and more comfortable routine, but as time does what she does, and life moves as she moves, that consistency will become your safe haven, the mundane your peace.

You'll find that you can breathe life into your days if you want to. You'll remind yourself that you are the sum of what you choose to repeat. You'll learn that tiny miracles are what the ordinary is made of. You'll step closer to the edge and bask in the beauty.

MAYBE WE SHOULD GIVE ALL THE FUCKS

My son waves goodbye to the dragonflies as we pass the threshold of our front door. I catch sight of shattered shell and pale-yellow dried yoke. Two finches chatter as they look on. I can hear the agony in their voices. In the yard, a female turtle searches for a place to lay her eggs, neck stretched, eyes wide. Yesterday, tornadoes ripped through my hometown. Later, I swear I felt my growing baby kick for the first time.

The weather is crisp for the cusp of summer,
a gift from the storm.
Tonight, the northern lights are visible in this
southern sky.

The world is changing, and yet she stays steady in her ways.
Nothing is promised.
Life rolls on.
The sun sets, but even nights can be beautiful.

WHEN I DIE

Give me to the earth-angels.
With their heads bowed in devotion,
with their steady, watchful eyes.
Lay me on the ground and let them prepare my body.
One last worship.
One final sacrifice.
Let me be as dignified as the buck quiet along the road,
as honored
as the coyote in the morning light.
Let me join them in re-creation,
reborn as wide, black wings painting
the evening sky.

MY POT OF GOLD

We sat on the back deck for hours, watched the lizards scurry along the wooden railing, lazily drank red wine mixed with orange juice and fresh fruit. It was one of those days that awoke as spring and matured into summer, the sky losing its crisp touch as moisture and heat filled her to the brim. You wore that smile that spells serenity. I was breathing softer than I ever had. Our son stripped down and splashed in the hose, his laughter clinging to each droplet flying through the air.

The sun on the water made dancing rainbows, and I knew
I'd found my pot of gold.

button poetry

ACKNOWLEDGEMENTS

Love and appreciation to:

My husband, for reading every poem and gently correcting every typo. There is nothing we can't trudge through – from misspellings to the end of the world – may we always manage to find joy along the way.

Evan, for showing me the true meaning of life. You are pure light.

Button Poetry, with special thanks to Sam and Tanesha for helping me believe that I do belong in their wonderful community.

ABOUT THE AUTHOR

Lauren E. Bowman is the author of three poetry collections, *The Evolution of a Girl* (Black Castle Media Group), *What I Learned from the Trees* (Button Poetry), and her latest, *Shapeshifter* (Button Poetry).

Lauren's work often delves into the intricate relationship between humans and nature, and how these often overlooked, everyday interactions affect us as individuals, families, and communities. She also focuses heavily on all facets of womanhood, including the shifting roles and definitions that we face as we change and age.

Being a full-time working mother and a part-time writer, Lauren pulls much of her inspiration from the capricious lives we tackle every day. Through sharing her own struggles with relationships and self-acceptance, she seeks to encourage others to learn from and rise above their own difficulties and doubts, and to find a place of reflection, empowerment, and growth.

AUTHOR BOOK RECOMMENDATIONS

Ephemera by Sierra DeMulder

Sierra's words grasp you from the very start and hold you close until the end. As warm and tender as a mother's arms, *Ephemera* details the often devastating, but always beautiful, intricacies of life.

Revenge Body by Rachel Wiley

Revenge Body is like confetti, it showers down on you and sticks for the world to see. Rachel's words are so bold and unforgiving, that you can't help but move through life a little differently – a pep in your step, a knife on your tongue.

You Better Be Lightning by Andrea Gibson

Andrea has a way with descriptions that leaves their poems burned on your eyes and in your lungs for days after reading. You'll find yourself searching and searching, only to arrive on your own doorstep, hands open, finally ready to step inside.

CREDITS

Assistant Editors
Marley Craine
Isabelle Miller

Book Photography
Emily Van Cook

Cover and Interior Design
Coral Black
Marley Craine

Distribution
SCB Distributors

Ebook Production
Siva Ram Maganti

Editor
Charley Eatchel

Publisher
Sam Van Cook

Publishing Operations Manager
TaneshaNicole Kozler

Publishing Operations Assistant
Charley Eatchel

Social Media and Marketing
Paloma Gomez
Catherine Guden
Eric Tu

OTHER BOOKS BY BUTTON POETRY

If you enjoyed this book, please consider checking out some of our others, below. Readers like you allow us to keep broadcasting and publishing. Thank you!

Natasha T. Miller, *Butcher*
Kevin Kantor, *Please Come Off-Book*
Ollie Schminkey, *Dead Dad Jokes*
Reagan Myers, *Afterwards*
L.E. Bowman, *What I Learned From the Trees*
Patrick Roche, *A Socially Acceptable Breakdown*
Rachel Wiley, *Revenge Body*
Ebony Stewart, *BloodFresh*
Ebony Stewart, *Home.Girl.Hood.*
Kyle Tran Myhre, *Not A Lot of Reasons to Sing, but Enough*
Steven Willis, *A Peculiar People*
Topaz Winters, *So, Stranger*
Darius Simpson, *Never Catch Me*
Blythe Baird, *Sweet, Young, & Worried*
Siaara Freeman, *Urbanshee*
Robert Wood Lynn, *How to Maintain Eye Contact*
Junious 'Jay' Ward, *Composition*
Usman Hameedi, *Staying Right Here*
Sean Patrick Mulroy, *Hated for the Gods*
Sierra DeMulder, *Ephemera*
Taylor Mali, *Poetry By Chance*
Matt Coonan, *Toy Gun*
Matt Mason, *Rock Stars*
Miya Coleman, *Cottonmouth*
Ty Chapman, *Tartarus*
Lara Coley, *ex traction*
DeShara Suggs-Joe, *If My Flowers Bloom*
Ollie Schminkey, *Where I Dry the Flowers*
Edythe Rodriguez, *We, the Spirits*
Topaz Winters, *Portrait of My Body as a Crime I'm Still Committing*
Zach Goldberg, *I'd Rather Be Destroyed*
Eric Sirota, *The Rent Eats First*
Neil Hilborn, *About Time*
Josh Tvrdy, *Smut Psalm*
Phil SaintDenisSanchez, *before & after our bodies*
Ebony Stewart, *WASH*

Available at buttonpoetry.com/shop and more!

BUTTON POETRY BEST SELLERS

FORTHCOMING BOOKS BY BUTTON POETRY

Najya Williams, *on a date with disappointment*
Daniel Elias Galicia, *Still Desert*
Hailey M. Tran, *an everyday occurrence*
Chelsea Guevara, *Cipota*
Meg Ford, *Wild/Hurt*
Jared Singer, *Forgotten Necessities*

Available at buttonpoetry.com/shop and more!